I0430945

How to Create and Deliver Effective Training Programs

Suggestions to help you get started

This book was Created for DataLAB, LLC. by
Robert J Schenck, Jr, MSEd
& Robert J Schenck III

Illustration by GC Rosenquist

Contents

FOREWORD **5**

A NOTE FROM MY DAD **6**

AN INTRODUCTION **9**

A. Employees need updated training on new policies and procedures 9

B. Need to improve employee skills: 9

C. Introductory training for new hires: 10

D. Regulatory requirements: 10

E. Employee morale: 11

F. Other reasons as requested by senior management: 12

IDENTIFYING NEEDS **14**

Top level management: 14

Supervisory personnel: 14

Regulatory changes, safety, etc: 15

Employee requests: 16

IDENTIFYING TRAINING MATERIALS **18**

Equipment Manufacturers: 18

Regulators: 18

State and Local Agencies: 19

Company Rules: 21

SUGGESTED DESIGN CONSIDERATIONS 22

Students: 22

Training Location: 24

Instructors: 24

COURSE MANAGEMENT 27

One final thought: 28

APPENDIX 30

RELEVANT LINKS 31

Continue the conversation with us: 31

Foreword

Thanks for checking out this short read to get you started on creating your training. My dad wrote this for me when I told him I was going to make an online class about hose to Side Hustle: Like a business. (Links in back with QR Codes to relevant pages)

My dad has been studying the education of adults for over 20 years. After retiring from the Sherriff's department where he worked in Emergency Management, he went to the local Community college and taught Emergency Management, Anti Terrorism and a few other courses to prepare the next generation of first responders. After retiring he got his Masters in Education from Northern Illinois University. I followed in his footsteps at NIU and got my BS in Business Administration.

After graduating I have done a number of varying careers across business and data. From insurance and investments, to food safety, and corporate property management, then to logistics and healthcare. All the while working with and teaching people about data.

I like to dig into the complex and make it simple for others, I hope this inspires you to do the same.

I'm blessed to have had all the support from both my parents. And I know some don't have the luck of having a dad like I do. So, in this, let me share the help I got from my dad, to help you on getting your next training going!

Get in touch with me over at DataLikeABusiness.com

A Note from my Dad

This book is intended to help you get started with your training project. Each situation will be different so you will need to adjust accordingly. Included here are certain key items that should be considered when starting and developing a training program.

Consider creating multiple courses if necessary, rather than cramming too much into your course. Keep in mind that students will probably differ greatly in terms of skills, needs, and so forth. Topics should be directly related to each other. It would be a bad idea to get too far off topic.

NOTE: If at any time you have a question on anything related to this book, feel free to contact us at:

Support@DataLikeABusiness.com .

Just send us an email and we will do what we can to help you. **If you need a reply, be sure to include your name, email address, and phone number, and the best time to call for your time zone. We will get back to you as soon as possible.** If Rob can't answer your question, he will forward it to me, and I will get back to you. I see him all the time...he's my son.

R. Schenck, Jr

Creating Training Programs

An Introduction

T
h
e
r
e
a
r
e
m
a
ny reasons why organizations may want or need to create training programs. How we go about creating training programs depends on many factors including the type of organization and its needs. In no particular order these will include:

A. Employees need updated training on new policies and procedures: Employees must be kept abreast of changes within the organization including policies, procedures, new equipment, and the like.

B. Need to improve employee skills: As technology advances employees need to be updated on it. Sometimes we encounter "we've always done it this way" but there are better and more efficient ways of doing a task. Explaining this to employees can help reduce resistance to the changes.

C. Introductory training for new hires: A Newly hired employee needs to understand his or her individual role and responsibilities as well as how they fit into the overall organizational structure. They need to understand that they are important to the success of the organization and are valued as employees. This is part of team building. Employees need to understand their individual roles as they apply to the overall organization and what is expected of them.

D. Regulatory requirements: Some tasks are governed by local, state, or federal regulations such as EPA, OSHA, and others. Good training programs, along with proper documentation will help here. Employees need to know, for example, when safety equipment is required, what equipment is needed, how to ensure the equipment is in good condition, and so forth. Insurance carriers, too, may have special requirements for certain situations and the employees need to be aware of that as well.

Documentation will include the date, time, and location of the training, employee's name and employee number, how much time was spent in training, and the results of tests if any are given. Included in the documentation is an outline of the course presented and any documents used as handouts. We also need to ensure that the training conforms to any regulations covering the organization.

E. Employeemorale

When Is Safety Equipment Required?

How Do We Ensure That Equipment Is In Good Condition?

: Sometimes employees will request training on a task, especially tasks that are new to them. Employees may also make suggestions on a better way to do something. After all, because they are the ones doing something they are often better equipped to make suggestions for improving how a task can be done. Any such suggestions should be evaluated by the appropriate management and the employee should be informed of the outcome. This helps to make the employee feel valuable to the organization.

F. Other reasons as requested by senior management: This can present problems to the supervisors of the employees. Upper management may not understand why something is done the way it is. If the request is valid then it is time to create training on the changes. If not, then the person making the request should be informed why it is not a good idea.

As mentioned earlier, documentation might be critical if something such as an accident occurs. Say, for example, an employee sustains a head injury on the job. Was he wearing a hard hat? What was he doing at the time of the accident? Was he following procedures correctly and were the procedures good or do they need updating? Obviously, safety of the employee should be of the utmost importance, but we need to ensure that we are doing things correctly. Employees, too, should feel empowered to ask, "where is your hard hat?" If that doesn't get compliance with policies and procedures it should be brought to the attention of supervisors for corrective action.

This is just one example of how important proper training, both initially and in service, can protect

not only the employee but the organization from liability and the loss of production. Documentation of training must be kept up to date and readily available in the time of need, even if solely for periodic review. In the long run, your training program for employees will enhance not only safety. But overall organizational performance.

Creating Training Programs
Identifying Needs

Identifying training needs is important. There are many factors that could be involved in identifying training needs. They could be both internal to the organization as well as outside organizations such as regulatory agencies or insurance carriers.

Top level management: These are the folks who determine what is to be done and with what priorities. Keep in mind that, while they are important decision makers, they may not fully understand exactly how tasks are assigned and completed. When they say they want new procedures, for example, lower-level supervisors and workers should be consulted to see if the changes are viable or not, or if a compromise can be reached. Remember to be respectful of top-level management so that a mutually agreed upon solution can be reached.

Supervisory personnel: These are usually longer-term employees whose job it is to oversee the day-to-day operations of the organization. They are valuable because they will have a better idea of how things are done

15

now as well as possible changes or improvements.

Regulatory changes, safety, etc: Regulators such as OSHA, EPA, and the like frequently come up with procedural changes. Often times this is due to something that happened elsewhere and is now being applied to your organization. While well intentioned they may be impractical in some instances. Still we need to comply with regulations, so we need to find a middle ground to both comply with regulations as well as fitting into the organization's way of doing things. This is not a simple task sometimes. Still we need to be prepared for mandated changes. For example, with hazardous materials or equipment there can be stringent legal requirements for their use and storage. Fire departments are often involved in the inspection of facilities for fire safety issues. They usually have fire codes that relate to organizations, and they can be a great source for help here.

Employee requests: Employees may occasionally ask for training on tasks, especially if they are new to the task. They may also identify specific areas where training is needed. It may be simply assigning a worker to a more senior employee to get the training. Or, depending on the situation, it might be better to offer formal classroom training.

Whatever the situation, it is always a good idea to check with the regulatory agency who came up with the required changes. Once you have developed a plan for the training you should present it to them to ensure you have met all of their requirements before you implement the plan in training. If something needs to be modified that's the time to do it. I call this "waterfowl linearity" which means you have all of your "ducks in a row" before you start the training. It might also be a good idea to check with your legal team if you have one so they can advise you on your situation.

Creating Training Programs

Identifying Training Materials

Depending on what you need to accomplish with your training program, there are many sources of information available to you. You just have to know where to look for it. Maybe someone in your organization is a member of a group of similar organizations or, at least, knows someone from another organization. That might be a source for you to draw upon. Here are a few suggestions:

Equipment Manufacturers: The folks who sold you equipment probably have someone who can give you advice or even training on their equipment. Not only is it good for their business but it can be good for yours as well. They may already have training materials you could use. An added benefit for you is the employees will learn how to not only use the equipment safely and properly but may also be able to identify problems before they become major issues.

Regulators: Many regulatory agencies like OSHA have training available for use. One advantage to this is their materials will comply with their regulations. You won't have to "reinvent the wheel".

State and Local Agencies: Many of these agencies have training programs available to the public if requested. Fire departments often have training on the use of fire extinguishers or First Aid/CPR and are willing to share it with you. That can make their job easier if something does happen. State level agencies are another source of information. In a recent tornado that struck an Amazon warehouse there was heavy damage to the building and several employees lost their lives. Had the warehouse management asked the state or even local emergency management officials for help before the incident the outcome could have been much different[1].

Company Rules: Sometimes company rules play into this equation. There is probably a reason for the company rules being used. Be careful of "we've always done it this way" though. The rules may have worked when the company was founded decades ago but maybe there is room for improvement. If that is the case, make the improvements before starting to plan the training.

Use your imagination and experience when deciding how to proceed. An Internet search just might turn up a program already available that you could adopt. Be aware, though, that these courses and materials can sometimes be costly. You might even be able to find books on the subject to give you some ideas to incorporate into your training. Be sure, though, to vet the source to ensure they are reliable and not some person who put something together.

Creating Training Programs

Suggested Design Considerations

Now it's time to get to the heart of what you are going to do. In graduate school in education we were taught to be a "guide on the side, not a sage on the stage". The idea behind this is the term "Andragogy". This term is used by those in the education or training of adults. Simply put it means "the art and science of helping adults learn". Adults, because of their age and experience, will have frames of reference when learning new things. Here are some things to consider when you are designing your training:

Students: They are the most important consideration in this process. Without them there wouldn't be a need for training in the first place. You probably will have little, if any, input into who they. Just be aware of who they are as much as possible. Things to consider are their ages, work experiences, time with the company and the tasks they are assigned. You should consider some of them might have difficulty in learning new concepts so monitor them closely. Ask questions to see if they are getting what you are saying or if you have to try a different approach. Language used in the delivery needs to be appropriate for what you are doing. Don't use jargon or technical language unless you are sure they will understand it. Remember they are human and should be treated with respect.

You've got to mesh the dernadyne into the ellipsoid so the globulate is even with the particulate...

Training Location: You may not have much control over where the training is conducted but there are some things to consider. The training room should be, as much as possible, clean, quiet, and comfortable. Be sure to plan for periodic breaks for bathroom use, coffee, lunch, and just being able to get up and move around. As the saying goes, "the mind will absorb only as much as the butt can tolerate". If the students are uncomfortable or the training room is too hot or too cold that can be a factor in the success of the training. If you have to conduct part of the training in the facility where there is noise from machinery and so forth be sure they can all hear you. This should be avoided, if at all possible, except perhaps for demonstrations. If you are using computer-based or self-study materials make sure the students can handle it, especially for computer-based training. Some students might not have the ability to do computer-based learning. If you find someone who can't do computer-based training you will have to find another solution.

Instructors: This is an area that requires careful attention. Not everyone is comfortable teaching a class in front of students. Whomever you select will, hopefully at least, have experience is similar situations. At the very least he or she should have a clear, pleasant, speaking voice and be able to speak plainly so the students can hear them. If it is necessary to bring in an outside person for all or part of the course keep these things in mind as well. Whomever you select as an instructor, he or she needs to understand what you are delivering. If an SME (subject matter expert) is required for all or part of the program the above will apply to him or her as well. Humor is okay and can be used occasionally. Just remember to keep it clean and don't over do it. Remember, you're not doing stand-up comedy.

Creating Training Programs

Course Management

Depending on your situation and what your goals are, you may want to consider the use of quizzes and tests. In doing this you will see how well your training was received by the students. Your primary goal should be to ensure your training was successful. If you feel something needs to be added this is the time to do it. Since this is a non-credit course, you should use quizzes and tests informally only to evaluate students' progress.

Students who complete the course should be given some kind of recognition of their accomplishments. This could be a certificate, letter, or something the students can keep for themselves. A copy should also be placed in their permanent HR records.

Managing the course is important. This begins with designing the training and ends when it is all finished. One good way to find out how well your training was received is to ask. Try to use of an end of course evaluation. This should be a brief, anonymous, questionnaire handed out to the students at the end before they are dismissed. Don't take them personally but rather evaluate what they say and adjust things if possible and necessary.

Once the course is completed and you have reviewed the feedback from the students you should review it with your boss or bosses. With proper preparation you will be successful.

One final thought: If you decide to use someone else as the instructor(s) it would be a good idea to create a train-the-trainer program. Your first step here is to have them take the course. Then, assign them a part of the program and have them present it as if they are giving the class. This way you can see how well they do and make corrections or changes in their presentations if needed. Stopping by while they are doing a class will also help you ensure the instructor is doing well.

G
O
O
D
L
U
C
K
W
I
T
H
Y
O
U
R
P
R
O
G
R
A

M!